Winning Ways for Early Childhood Professionals

Being a Professional

Gigi Schweikert

Name: ______________________________

Date: ______________________________

Redleaf Press®
www.redleafpress.org
800-423-8309

Also in the Winning Ways series from Redleaf Press

Supporting Positive Behavior
Responding to Behavior
Guiding Challenging Behavior
Parterning with Families
Becoming a Team Player
Understanding Infants
Understanding Toddlers and Twos
Understanding Preschoolers
Being a Supervisor

Published by Redleaf Press
10 Yorkton Court
St. Paul, MN 55117
www.redleafpress.org

First edition 2012
Cover design by Jim Handrigan
Cover photograph © iStockphoto.com / jo unruh
Interior design by Erin Kirk New
Printed in the United States of America

Library of Congress Cataloging-in-Publication Data
Schweikert, Gigi, 1962–
Winning ways for early childhood professionals : being a professional / Gigi Schweikert.
p. cm.
ISBN 978-1-60554-001-6
1. Early childhood educators—Professional relationships. I. Title.
LB1775.6.S38 2012
372.21—dc23

2011026612

Printed on acid-free paper

U16-05

Contents

From the Desk of Gigi Schweikert

This is me presenting.

Dear Winning Ways Reader
(and Early Childhood Professional),

Like many of you, I have been working with young children all my life, since I was eighteen months old and my brother David was born—the life of a firstborn with a couple siblings. Actually, I was nine when I started officially working with children. I set up a summer camp in my backyard for the neighborhood kids. Parents paid fifty cents a day per child. Good deal for them!

Teaching young children has always been my passion. It's all I ever wanted to do. I never really thought about what it meant to be a professional until my family continued to ask me after I had graduated college, "When are you going to get a real job?" I was a toddler teacher at the time. I thought working with young children and helping to mold the brains of the next generation was a "real job"—it didn't matter if my family thought differently.

But in fairness to my family and other people who don't always understand what we do, I started thinking maybe there is something to being a *professional.* And maybe we have more control over how others perceive us than we think. Do we act like professionals? Dress like professionals? Speak like professionals? I could do a better job sometimes. How about you?

Caring for and educating children is one of the most important professions, and I think it's our responsibility to educate others that we *are* professionals. This Winning Ways book is full of ideas to help you be the professional you really are. After you've read the book, I'd love to hear your ideas about how you exhibit professionalism and show others we do have a "real job," one that really does make a difference. Send me your thoughts at www.gigischweikert.com.

Children deserve our winning ways,

Introduction

Are You an Early Childhood Professional?

You may be thinking, "What is an early childhood professional?" Perhaps you refer to yourself as a preschool teacher, a child care provider, a family child care provider, a nursery school teacher, or just a plain teacher. An early childhood professional is anyone who cares for and educates young children, typically newborns to early schoolagers. Let's not forget substitutes, directors, coordinators, and all the other titles people use in our field. They're all early childhood professionals too.

Have you not really considered yourself a professional? Many in early childhood education don't see themselves as professionals, and that's no surprise, given that society often views those in the field as babysitters or pseudo teachers. Our wages certainly don't match up to the compensation of other professional jobs, and many people just don't understand what we do. A lot of them think we play all day. If they only knew.

Contrary to what some may think, you are a professional, and parts of your role as a professional include feeling like a professional and acting like a professional. It's difficult to feel competent and important when others don't see you that way, but perhaps if more people in the early childhood field claimed the title of professional, consistently demonstrated professional behavior, and worked to advocate for the field, society would begin to view us that way. Are you ready for the challenge?

What Makes a Professional?

There are many factors that determine professionalism in any field:

- How you present yourself to others through your appearance and communication

- Your knowledge of the field
- The quality of your work
- The relationships you develop with others
- Your work ethic
- Your determination and dedication
- Most important, your attitude

Everyone in early childhood education is passionate about working with children. Now's the time to get passionate about how to present yourself to others and represent the early childhood field to society.

Using This Book

Winning Ways for Early Childhood Professionals: Being a Professional is divided into six key steps that lay the framework for professionalism in the field. Whether tomorrow is your first day on the job or you've been teaching for twenty years, this book can provide a little help. Check out the sections below and look for ways that you and others in your program can be more professional.

1. Look the Part
2. Act the Part
3. Know Your Stuff
4. Be on the Job
5. Save the Comments
6. Take Care

SELF-ASSESSMENT

Are You a True Early Childhood Professional?

Take a quick self-assessment to see how well you are doing as a true early childhood professional. As you read each of the statements below and circle the frequency that best describes your appearance, actions, and attitudes, be honest with yourself. How you think you present yourself to others and how you think you act are not always what others see or experience. In other words, perception is reality. Regardless of your intent, how others view you or interpret your actions is just as important as what you intend.

Knowing that perception is reality, you may even want to have someone at work assess you as well. Having a coworker or supervisor assess you can be a bit uncomfortable, since no one likes to hear that she needs to change. Start with your self-assessment and then gain the confidence to ask someone else to assess you. You can't change what you don't know, and it's so hard to view yourself objectively.

1 I maintain a professional appearance by dressing appropriately and presenting myself in a professional manner.

Always Usually Sometimes Never

2 I act professionally by being on time, maintaining confidentiality, and smiling.

Always Usually Sometimes Never

3 I am knowledgeable about child development and early childhood education and continue to learn new things.

Always Usually Sometimes Never

4 I am prepared for work by being physically present and mentally engaged.

Always Usually Sometimes Never

5 I have a good attitude at work and show my positive attitude through my actions and conversations.

Always Usually Sometimes Never

6 I realize that my job requires me to care for children and their families.

Always Usually Sometimes Never

Six Steps to Being a Pro

Even if you circled "Always" be sure to read the corresponding step—there's always something to learn and improve on. Refer back to your completed self-assessment form as you explore the six steps to becoming an early childhood professional.

STEP 1

Look the Part

1

I maintain a professional appearance by dressing appropriately and presenting myself in a professional manner.

- Always
- Usually
- Sometimes
- Never

Is Your Appearance at Work Professional?

Just how professional can you look when you spend your days sitting on the floor with children, making playdough, painting, changing diapers, and serving food? Dressing in a comfortable style that allows for active movement and messy activities doesn't mean you can't look professional. Whether you like it or not, others tend to quickly judge you based on your outward appearance. A strong professional look gives early childhood educators the credibility they deserve. It probably wouldn't make sense for you to wear business attire while working with children, but wearing ill-fitting sweats covered in food stains doesn't make sense either; such a look robs you of your credibility.

Do You Look the Part?

So how do you dress professionally yet in a way that allows you to actively engage with little ones? The standards for professional appearance will vary based on your program's culture. Your administrators, along with other governing bodies such as your board or employee sponsor, will help determine guidelines for acceptable dress and appearance.

Does all this talk about dress seem a little silly? Not when you consider that others are more likely to treat you like a professional when you look like a professional. Do you dress to impress? You should.

The Appropriate Look

It's probably fair to say that no one is trying to look inappropriate, yet in today's culture, where a myriad of clothing styles exists, how do we know what is acceptable?

Here are some tips to help you decide.

Clothing

- Remember that you are dressing for work.
- Make sure that your clothing is modest, not revealing.
- Ask your director for guidance if you have questions.
- Err on the side of more professional than less professional.
- Choose simple clothing.
- Go for more classic styles instead of the current fad.
- Select clothing that allows you to move easily and comfortably.

Jeans and Sweats

Are jeans considered professional? Your professionalism is not determined solely by your appearance; how you act has a greater long-range impact on whether you are seen as professional or not. Many programs feel that jeans are inappropriate for professionals to wear. If you take your cues from the business world, then jeans don't usually have a place in your work wardrobe. Consider jeans on Friday or once a month. If jeans are considered professional at your program all the time, that's okay too.

What about sweats? Personally, I don't think anyone can make sweats look professional. Save them for the gym or lounging at home.

A professional look doesn't include the following. Here are some early childhood fashion don'ts:

- Don't wear dirty or stained clothing.
- Don't wear torn or worn clothing, even if it's supposed to look that way.
- Don't let your undergarments show through your clothes or when you bend down or bend over.

- Don't wear ill-fitting clothing that can catch on furniture or equipment.
- Don't wear clothing that fits too tightly.
- Don't wear clothing that has loose buttons, sequins, or other small pieces that can fall off and become a choking hazard for children.
- Don't wear clothing that is revealing. You do a lot of bending over and reaching up. Stretch up and over before you leave the house to make sure your body is properly covered.

Uniforms and Smocks

In some centers, early childhood professionals wear uniforms or smocks. Uniforms and smocks can be professional. Think about the uniforms of nurses, doctors, and sports figures. A uniform may consist of a colored shirt and pair of pants, or a shirt with the center logo or emblem. Smocks are typically worn to protect a teacher's clothes and to identify her as an employee. Here are some of the advantages to wearing uniforms and smocks:

- They create a distinctive, professional look.
- They enable families and visitors to quickly identify employees.
- They make selecting appropriate clothing easier for the teacher.
- They protect the teacher's personal clothes from damage.
- They ensure that an employee's clothing is appropriate.

Here are some of the disadvantages that early childhood professionals have noted:

- Uniforms don't allow teachers to express personal clothing style.
- Uniforms are less professional.
- Uniforms must be kept clean and ready for work the next day.
- Uniforms require additional expense.

Shoes

Ever try to catch a preschooler on the run or a toddler darting for the parking lot? Having on a pair of "sensible shoes," as my husband would call them, is an early childhood must. You spend a great deal of time on the go, inside and out. When it comes to shoes, safety counts. Just remember that sensible doesn't necessarily mean unattractive.

What's the best shoe for the job? Preferably a sneaker or something like it. With so many styles to choose from, you'll have no problem finding something. What are you looking for? Shoes that

- Provide foot support because you are moving about
- Have a sole that prevents slipping
- Have a soft sole to avoid hurting little fingers on the floor
- Fit well
- Are flat or have a low heel
- Cover the entire foot

What shoes should you save for after work?

- High heels
- Flip-flops and sandals
- Shoes with slippery soles

Name Tags

Name tags can add a great deal of professionalism and benefit to any program. Relationships build more quickly when people can call others by name. It's your job to know the names of all the children in your care and their parents, and you want them to know your name too. Name tags make that easy. Name tags can also

- Identify you as an employee
- Help other people learn your name more easily
- Indicate your job by including your title
- Highlight years of experience, degrees, or accreditation
- Provide sight words for children

Nails

In early childhood education, your hands are moving as fast as your feet. You need to be able to quickly and efficiently carry out the responsibilities of your job. That means constantly using your hands and constantly washing them. Although nails have become a fashion accessory, consider the following for work. You want nails that are

- Clean
- Short enough to allow you to quickly perform your job responsibilities such as zipping coats and fastening buttons
- Short enough for you to easily clean under them at work

Long, manicured nails can be beautiful, but consider their disadvantages. They can

- Scratch children unintentionally
- Collect dirt, food particles, and bodily fluids
- Break or bend more easily, hurting you
- Leave nail polish chips in food or on the floor

Jewelry

Jewelry is not only decorative, it can also be symbolic—for example, wedding rings, school rings, and religious symbols. In an industry that celebrates diversity, jewelry can be a way to express cultural heritage. Is there a place for jewelry at work as an early childhood professional? Of course. Again, safety for the child and for you is the main concern. Use these ideas when selecting jewelry to wear at work:

- Since you wash your hands so often, minimize rings and bracelets.
- Avoid jewelry that can easily scratch children.
- Consider the age of the children with whom you are working. Infants and toddlers may grab or pull jewelry that dangles from your ears or neck.
- Avoid jewelry that can break easily, such as a strand of beads. They may pose a choking hazard for children.
- Leave jewelry that you do not want to lose at home.

Makeup and Perfume or Cologne

Wearing makeup is a personal preference. Apply a minimal amount for on the job. If you are a big kid-kisser, consider whether to wear lipstick. Lipstick kiss marks, if not removed, can look like bruises or injuries on children. Children can also be allergic to makeup.

Lots of smells are associated with early childhood education, some good, others not. It's certainly important and professional to smell good, but adults and children are often allergic to strong perfume or cologne. With infants and toddlers, you may not even know of potential allergies. Use perfume or cologne sparingly.

Hair

Hair should be clean, well groomed, and off your face. If you are constantly pushing your hair away from your face while you are working, then pull it back. Programs have different policies about hair when you are serving food. Some centers, health departments, and state licensing regulations require you to wear a hairnet or hat. This may include when you are feeding infants or serving children in the classroom. Ask your supervisor about requirements.

Hygiene

Working with young children requires physical exertion and much activity. Remember that good hygiene, keeping yourself and your clothes clean and washed, requires daily effort. You can look professional and not smell professional. Cultural norms about hygiene differ. However, since you are caring for young children, your hygiene standards have the potential to affect the health and safety of those around you. Do not be offended if your supervisor or another employee offers to educate you about the hygiene standards in your program.

Body Art, Tattoos, and Piercings

Although tattoos and piercings are more common today, they are not always considered professional. Let your program's culture guide this aspect of your personal appearance. If you have questions, ask your supervisor.

What Does an Early Childhood Professional Look Like?

There's not one right way for an early childhood professional to look professional, but it's interesting to note that most professions have a look. Think about it: business people, nurses, and artists all have a look. We certainly don't want to generalize about any group of people, but norms of appearance are common in most fields. Is the lack of "What an early childhood educator looks like" a deterrent to professional credibility?

Perhaps you need to pay more attention to first impressions and how you present yourself physically. Looking good is only a small part of being professional and gaining credibility. Acting professionally helps you hang on to that credibility. Act the Part is the next step to professionalism.

OPTIMIZE YOUR KNOWLEDGE

1 List three professions other than early childhood education and describe the **professional appearance** of each occupation.

1 ______________________________

2 ______________________________

3 ______________________________

winning ways

2 Summarize the benefits of wearing a **name tag**.

____

____

____

____

3 Explain how inappropriate dress and appearance can undermine your **credibility** and that of the early childhood education field.

____

____

____

____

STEP 2

Act the Part

2

I act professionally by being on time, maintaining confidentiality, and smiling.

- Always
- Usually
- Sometimes
- Never

How Do Professionals Act?

How should early childhood professionals act? Certainly common behavior constitutes professionalism in every occupation. Some of that behavior is common courtesy that everyone should exhibit, whether they are at work or not. Do you ever feel that everyone could be a little nicer?

You have a unique and rewarding job in which singing silly songs or wearing funny hats is hardly considered unprofessional—it's part of the job. But your work as an early childhood professional is not all fun and games. There is a serious side of your job that requires uncompromising professional behavior. Early childhood professionals have a great responsibility to act appropriately. Why? Because you care for and educate young children. You not only provide for their health and safety; you also educate them with your actions. The children are watching you, and so are their families. Are you a good role model?

Do You Act the Part?

Acting professionally takes consistent effort, and doing the right thing is not always easy. Whether you are a newcomer to the field bringing enthusiasm and energy or a veteran providing patience and experience, how you interact with the children, their families, other staff, and your communities determines whether others see you as a professional. Are you acting appropriately and representing the early childhood education field well? You should be. Here are some of the things an early childhood professional should do.

Be on Time

In an industry where the care of children depends on your physical presence, you cannot be late. Punctuality is key to your professional success and the safety of the children. Yes, there are times in your career when you will be tardy, but consistent lateness is unacceptable. For ideas on how to get to work on time, check out step 7 in *Winning Ways for Early Childhood Professionals: Becoming a Team Player*, another booklet in this series.

Get Enough Sleep

Everyone knows what happens to young children when they don't get enough sleep: they become cranky, impatient, and easily frustrated. This happens to adults too. The physical and emotional demands of your job make being well rested essential to your success.

Be Polite

A simple "please" or "thank you" goes a long way. You expect children to learn this behavior, but do you exhibit it yourself? Being polite and courteous to others takes greater effort on your part, but make it a priority. Politeness catches. There is no place in your work for rude behavior, which unfortunately catches too.

Be Friendly

You don't have to be friends with everyone at work, but you do have to be friendly. What do friendly people do? Friendly people

- Acknowledge the presence of others
- Show genuine interest in others
- Help others without being asked
- Demonstrate common courtesies, such as opening a door for someone
- Smile at others
- Enjoy their jobs
- Don't allow little things to bother them
- Share their resources
- Are polite

Remember Names

You certainly don't have difficulty remembering the names of the children you teach, but committing adults' names to memory can be harder to do. As a professional, you should know the names of all of the staff in your classroom and all of the parents. Ideally, you should know the names of everyone you work with and their families. That may not be possible if your program is extremely large. Calling others by name is not only professional but good customer service. It's easy to tell when someone uses that false, very exaggerated, "Hi," that indicates he has forgotten your name. If you are seeking to form relationships with parents in order to better care for their children, the very least you can do is call the parents by name.

Being Friendly All the Time

Ever encounter someone you feel is not too friendly? What do you do? Sometimes the best way to get others to be friendly is to be friendly yourself. As a professional, you need to be friendly even when others aren't.

Smile

Fewer things are more rewarding to an early childhood educator than the toothless grin of an infant or the I-can-do-it smile of a preschooler. People love to see children smile, and children do it effortlessly—they are amazed by the world and the people in it, and that makes them smile.

Some adults rarely smile. For many, it's uncomfortable to smile. What happened? Did someone tell them their smile was funny or their teeth were crooked? Were they hit too many times by that favorite adult phrase "What are you smiling at?" Was smiling socialized out of you? It's okay to smile; in fact, smiling is part of being a professional. If you can smile at kids, you can smile at adults. Give it a try.

Have a Sense of Humor

Professionals take serious things seriously but also know when to laugh. Often it takes laughing to get through the serious stuff. Having a sense of humor doesn't mean making fun of others; it means making light of yourself.

Do You Read Center Communications That Are Directed to You?

When someone questions your job performance, it's easy to respond, "I didn't know." In many situations, you may not have known. How your supervisors communicate to you is their responsibility. Your responsibility as a professional is to learn as much as you can about your center and your job, and that means reading all communication given to you. It also means asking questions when you don't understand the information or when information is lacking.

Is there a big stack of stuff you need to read at work? Are there e-mails you need to respond to or voice mails that need answers? The technology age is wonderful because it brings you lots of information quickly. However, it can sometimes seem to deliver too much information. If you feel that you are receiving too much information, speak with your supervisor. Regardless of the volume of communication, you are still responsible for reading the information and responding appropriately.

What to Do with Center Communications

1. **Read.** Read all center correspondence and communication given to you.
2. **Learn.** Learn the information that is communicated.
3. **Ask.** Ask questions when you don't understand or need more information.
4. **Do.** Do what is requested in the communication, such as fill out a form or follow a policy.

What Type of Communication Can You Expect?

The amount of information you receive may feel overwhelming. Take a look at the list below.

- Staff handbooks
- Benefit information
- Memos
- Newsletters
- Performance appraisals
- Licensing standards
- Accreditation standards
- Company policies
- Curriculum ideas and forms
- Health and safety information
- Evacuation procedures
- Tracking sheets on individual children

Is there anything you could really eliminate? Probably not—and this is just a partial list. Some of the information in these communications is intended to be used as references. Should you really read through the entire state licensing requirements or other large volumes of information? Someone in your program has to, and that may be the director, but the more information you know, the better. We'll talk about knowledge in the next step, Know Your Stuff. At the very least, you should read your employee or staff handbook from cover to cover. Have you read your staff manual? Every page?

Read the Walls

Check out any early childhood program, and you'll see lots of information posted on the walls: procedures above changing tables, hand-washing instructions over sinks, a list of children's allergies in the food service area, and bulletin boards galore. Early childhood professionals even post things in the bathroom. Take some time to read the walls.

Do You Maintain Confidentiality?

Maintaining confidentiality is a crucial aspect of professionalism. In many occupations, state and federal laws bind and ensure people's right to privacy. When someone breaches your confidentiality, it feels almost as if you have been robbed. And in a way you have; someone has taken your private information and given it to others.

How do you handle confidentiality in early childhood education? No doubt you need a great deal of knowledge and information in order to care for and educate children. Most of that information is about the general care of children, but some of it is specific to a child, her family, or your coworkers. How do you know what information to share with others and what to keep confidential?

- Realize that you do not need to know everything about a child and his family in order to care for that child.
- Trust that the administrator of your program will share with you the information that is necessary to do your job well.
- Honor information that your supervisor deems confidential by not sharing it with anyone, even family and friends.
- Report any information you hear that has the potential to put a child or adult in danger, even if the person who tells you says, "Don't tell anyone."
- Refer individuals who ask you for confidential information to the director.
- Stop confidential information from spreading by confronting those who breach confidentiality.
- Use confidential information to help, not judge, a child, family, or coworker.

What Are the Early Childhood Education Behavior Don'ts?

I've addressed many of the professional do's of acting the part. Now it's time to point out some of the early childhood professional don'ts. Eliminate these behaviors, and you're well on your way to being more professional.

Don't Break the Rules

The policies and guidelines in your program are there for a reason, for example, how food is handled, who can be alone with children. It's certainly okay to question rules and discuss whether they should be updated or even changed, but until they are it's your responsibility to follow and enforce them. The rules are for everyone. No one is above the rules.

Don't Use Profanity

You can express yourself without using inappropriate language. It's not funny, and there is no place for it in the work environment. Foul language around children is grounds for termination, and inappropriate talk around adults is just as bad. Being professional requires speaking appropriately.

Don't Make Inappropriate Comments or Jokes

Having a sense of humor is a workplace must, but making comments or jokes at the expense of others is wrong. Celebrate the diversity of the children and staff. Comments or jokes that are racist, sexist, or hateful in any way should not be tolerated. In some cases, they can even be viewed as criminal. Everyone can take a lesson in thinking before speaking.

Don't Talk on the Phone or Text during Work

Before you start work, put your cell phone away. If need to make or receive a personal call, do so at lunch or on your break. It has become more acceptable to check your phone while talking to others in social settings, but it is not okay to use your cell phone while you are working. Your complete attention needs to be directed to the children and your job.

Don't Make Inappropriate Gestures

Overt hand gestures may convey inappropriate messages. Those have no place at work or anywhere else, for the matter. But more subtle gestures and body language can be just as unprofessional. Make sure you are not pointing your finger at children or others, rolling your eyes, placing your hands on your hips, or frowning to convey frustration and anger. If you are feeling any of those emotions, take a minute to cool down and then express your thoughts appropriately.

Don't Eat or Drink in Front of the Children

Unless you are eating what the children are having or you are sitting with them and everyone has a lunch from home, you should not be consuming anything in front of the children that they cannot have themselves. Imagine someone having ice cream while you are eating green beans. That's just not fair.

Don't Bring Hot Beverages around the Children

Most of you love your cup of coffee, but java and other hot drinks can seriously burn children. Enjoy your coffee before you go into the classroom.

Don't Smoke on School Property

Everyone knows that smoking is not good for you and that secondhand smoke is also dangerous. You should never smoke around the children, but smoking elsewhere on program property sets a bad example for children and others. If you do smoke before or during the workday, wear a smoking smock that covers your clothes and take it off before returning to the children. Wash your hands and brush your teeth. The smell of smoke should not be associated with your loving care. You are a role model. Seek help and give up smoking.

Don't Watch Television or Listen to Personal Music

Yes, music for the children is fine, and occasional DVDs may be allowed in your center, but watching television or listening to personal music in the classroom is not. The music you choose for children to listen to should be age appropriate, not too loud, and played for a purpose, not simply for background sound. Wearing any type of headset while watching the children inhibits your ability to supervise them appropriately.

Don't Have a Bad Attitude

Early childhood education is demanding and challenging. You will have tough days, but your positive attitude can help you through even the most difficult situations. Be open to new ideas and change. Professionals have a can-do attitude.

Looking the part and acting the part are the first two steps to professionalism. What's next? Having experience and knowledge in your field. Do you know your stuff?

OPTIMIZE YOUR KNOWLEDGE

1 List some of the behaviors that you find **unacceptable** in an employee when you are a customer (for example, a diner at a restaurant, a patient at a doctor's office, or a customer at the mall.)

____

____

____

____

2 Name the **common courtesies** that you feel all early childhood professionals should exhibit.

3 Explain why a tardy teacher can create a **safety problem** in early childhood programs.

STEP 3

Know Your Stuff

3

I am knowledgeable about child development and early childhood education and continue to learn new things.

- Always
- Usually
- Sometimes
- Never

What Do Early Childhood Professionals Do?

Early childhood professionals care for and educate young children. Do you need special training to do these? Contrary to those who think that your job is something "anyone can do" or "simply babysitting," it takes a special kind of nurturing and patient person to work with young children. It takes a great deal of training and education. Are there teachers who are just born to work with young children? Sure, but even they are not exempt from learning more about how children develop and grow. No matter how much education or experience you have, you can always learn more. The best early childhood professionals are always seeking new and better ways to help children. In some ways, they are like children themselves: always exploring, always searching. Are you eager to learn more about your job? You should be!

What Do Early Childhood Professionals Need to Know?

So, would you agree that adults who keep learning help children to learn better? The most important part of being a professional is knowing and learning all you can about your field. You need to know your stuff. What are the basic competencies you need to get started? Some of the things you need to know are

Child development. How do children grow and learn?

Curriculum. What will children learn?

Good Enough Never Is

The phrase "good enough never is" is one of my favorite lessons from Jim Greenman. Jim wrote many books about children and the environments that best foster learning (and childhood). Part of our humanness makes us feel comfortable and content to do things the way they've always been done, to think "this is good enough." Now, sometimes you don't want to change things, such as the fundamental concepts of children learning through play or the need for active, hands-on learning, but why not explore better ways to make active learning happen?

Imagine if today's medical professionals simply accepted the health care standards of forty years ago, and thought that the stuff they did forty years ago was good enough. You wouldn't have laparoscopic surgery or more effective cancer medications and anesthesia. Think about how that might affect you or someone you know. The goal of the physicians doesn't change; they want to help reduce the risk of people becoming injured or ill and heal them when they are. Their goal doesn't change, just their methods.

That's what you have to do as an early childhood professional: maintain your goals of caring for and educating young children while finding ways to do both better. And that means knowing your stuff.

Teaching techniques. How do you motivate and encourage each child to learn?

Classroom management and discipline strategies. How do you help children to socialize and learn acceptable behavior?

Child assessment. How do you assess each child's learning and development so you can help all children succeed?

Teamwork. How do you work well with other adults?

Family partnerships. How do you build relationships with families so the child benefits?

Health and safety. How do you keep children healthy and safe?

And those are just the beginning. Are you expected to know everything when you start your job? Absolutely not. Even those with advanced degrees and experience have a steep learning curve when they begin working in a new program.

How Much Stuff Do You Know?

Everyone comes to the profession with different knowledge and experience. The training you bring to the job is important, but your desire to keep learning is even more critical. Knowing your stuff includes

1. The knowledge and education you bring to the job
2. Your on-the-job experience and training
3. Your desire and commitment to continuous learning and training

Education

Some who have been in the early childhood field may not have formal degrees. Years ago, fewer college programs were available in this field. Is having a college degree essential to work with young children? For those who have twenty years of experience, maybe not, but for those just starting out, a formal education provides many of the skills necessary for becoming a good teacher. And remember—it's never too late to go back to school! Here are some of the credentials that early childhood professionals may have:

- CDA—Child Development Associate
- Associate Degree, or higher, in Early Childhood Education
- Associate Degree, or higher, in Child Development
- Associate Degree, or higher, in Family Studies
- Associate Degree, or higher, in Early Childhood Special Education
- Associate Degree, or higher, in Elementary Education with concentration in Early Childhood Education
- Associate Degree, or higher, in a field other than Early Childhood Education

Keep on Learning

A formal degree is a great first step to higher-quality teaching, but a commitment to continuous learning is even more important. Do you have a positive attitude toward learning, or do you sometimes suffer from "I know-it-all?" Take the following self-assessment and discover your attitude toward learning.

Your Attitude toward Learning

Your attitude toward continuous learning is just as important as your current knowledge. What's your learning quotient? Circle your answers then add up your score.

1 I am eager to learn new things about early childhood education. I sign up for workshops, read articles, and try new ideas in my classroom.

Always · 3 Usually · 2 Sometimes · 1 Never · 0

2 I am realistic about my current abilities. I don't think I can do it all by myself. I am not ashamed to ask others for help.

Always · 3 Usually · 2 Sometimes · 1 Never · 0

3 I am truthful about my current knowledge base. I don't pretend to know things I don't and I am not embarrassed by my degree or experience.

Always · 3 Usually · 2 Sometimes · 1 Never · 0

4 I am open minded and realize "good enough never is." I don't say things like "This is the way we do it here."

Always · 3 Usually · 2 Sometimes · 1 Never · 0

5 I ask questions when I don't understand or need more information. I am not embarrassed when I don't know something. When I don't know, I am not too lazy to find out.

Always · 3 Usually · 2 Sometimes · 1 Never · 0

6 I am open to change. I support change by not complaining or grumbling.

Always · 3 Usually · 2 Sometimes · 1 Never · 0

7 I seek new learning opportunities. I use the staff library to get new ideas, or I observe other teachers at work.

Always · 3 Usually · 2 Sometimes · 1 Never · 0

8 I attend workshops and trainings. I go to at least the minimum numbers of workshops required by my program and usually more.

Always · 3 Usually · 2 Sometimes · 1 Never · 0

9 I share my experience and skills with others in the field. I give mini workshops at my program or do special projects in a class other than my own.

Always · 3 Usually · 2 Sometimes · 1 Never · 0

10 I stay current in the field. I know about legislation on early childhood education and current research on how children learn best.

Always · 3 Usually · 2 Sometimes · 1 Never · 0

11 I collect, save, and organize the information I learn so that I can use it as a reference for myself and others.

Always · 3 Usually · 2 Sometimes · 1 Never · 0

12 I ask others how well I am performing. I am not afraid to hear what others think of my performance. This includes other staff, families, administrators, and even the children.

Always · 3 Usually · 2 Sometimes · 1 Never · 0

What's Your Learning Quotient?

If you scored 36–30, you are a Sponge. Soak up any more information, and your brain might explode. Keep on learning, you're doing great, but remember not to overwhelm children or other adults with your many new ideas and enthusiasm.

If you scored 29–23, you are a Paper Towel. You have a healthy attitude toward learning more about the field and staying current. Concentrate on improving your weaker areas and think about how you can share your knowledge with others.

If you scored 22–12, you are a Cotton Ball. You're soft and comfortable but need to step up your learning a bit. Don't be afraid to venture out of your comfort zone.

If you scored 11–0, you are a cotton swab. You can't suck up a lot of knowledge with a cotton swab. Maybe you're in a learning rut. Start taking some baby steps to learn more about early childhood education. Doing so will help you and the children.

Moving through a Learning Rut

There are lots of reasons why you or someone you're working with may not be eager to learn more about early childhood education:

- You may have been in the field so long that you feel as if you know how to do it!
- You may have been in the field so long that you've lost a little of that ECE passion and spark.
- You may be new to the field, and you're overwhelmed. You feel as if you need to just practice the skills you have before learning more.
- You may have had some new ideas that didn't work well. You're afraid of failing.
- You may have a life outside of work and just don't have time to take classes or go to workshops.
- You may go to training sessions but feel they are often boring or uninteresting.

16 Ways to Push through a Learning Rut

Any of those sound like you? Everyone goes through learning ruts, but you have to push beyond them. Here are some ideas to get you started:

1. **Change your attitude.** Have an attitude that you can learn something from everyone or every experience.
2. **Think like a child.** Learning isn't a chore to children. It's as natural as breathing for them and a joy. Try to see the world from a child's point of view.
3. **Realize that no one knows it all.** You may have been in the field for years or have just received your PhD, but either way, those who know a lot usually realize that the more they learn, the more they have to learn.
4. **Take small steps toward a big goal.** Learning anything new can be overwhelming to adults. People usually don't like change. Take small steps, one workshop, one class, or one article at a time.
5. **Seek knowledge from many sources.** Learning doesn't just happen in an ECE course or in a workshop. Knowledge also comes from watching others and learning from our mistakes.

6 Use the stuff you learn. It doesn't help the quality of care and education that you provide the children if you never use what you've learned. Give it a try!

7 Teach what you know to someone else. When you teach something you know to another, that person benefits and you gain a deeper understanding of the information.

8 Relate the new information to old information. Learning new ideas doesn't always mean throwing out the old. New information can enhance the work you are already doing.

9 Discuss ideas with others. Have productive conversations and meetings in which you and others talk about ideas and how to effectively use them. It's a great way to energize your learning and passion for the field.

10 Join professional organizations. Local, state, and national organizations offer conferences that give you the most current information on early childhood education research, legislation, and practices. It's also fun to hang out with others who are doing the same job.

11 Attend conferences. Whether they last one day or a few days, ECE conferences are wonderful for getting out of the learning rut. Expect to learn one or two new ideas you can apply to your job. Don't be disappointed by presenters or topics that you didn't enjoy. (There are different styles and expectations. You'll find some are more to your liking than others.)

12 Read. Read professional journals, but don't forget to read the local newspaper and books about the hobbies you enjoy. You'll find new ideas that you can apply to your job just about everywhere.

13 Keep a list of your professional development. Write down the books you read or make a copy of articles. Keep a journal of some of the key points you learn on the job or in a course. Make a list of the workshops you attend. You'll be amazed and inspired by all the opportunities you take advantage of. That's professionalism.

14 Eliminate the excuses. There is no perfect time to start a course or sign up for a conference. If you have the will, you can figure out a way to go. In many cases, you can also find funding.

15 Take chances. You might fail when you try something new and you might not, but you will never know if you don't give it a chance.

16 Persevere. Push through boredom, procrastination, and interruptions. If you set your mind on reading an article, read it through to the end.

Sources of Learning

- Colleges and universities
- Formal courses
- Other people
- Staff trainings
- Workshops
- Books
- Articles
- On-the-job experience
- Performance appraisals
- Visits to other programs
- Mentors
- Partners
- Meetings
- Conferences

Do You Actively Participate in Workshops and Trainings?

Early childhood education requires that you participate in many training sessions and program events. Orientation is usually your first taste of employer-sponsored training. If you have worked in your program for a few years, retake the orientation class and reread the information that new employees receive. You'll learn a lot.

Since your job's first responsibility is providing coverage for the children, most of your meetings and trainings may be at night or on the weekend. Sometimes it's hard to get excited about attending training when you have worked all day, but professionals are always eager to learn more about their jobs.

Do you convey a positive attitude at trainings and workshops, or does your behavior indicate "I'd rather be home"? You may want to be at home, but don't show it. Get involved, and you may actually enjoy yourself. More important, you may learn something.

Getting the Most out of Trainings and Meetings

Be an effective participant:

- Know what the session is about.
- Be prepared to take notes.
- Be mentally present and pay attention.
- Actively listen.
- Ask questions.
- Don't have side conversations with others.
- Contribute your ideas when asked. Don't be afraid to speak up.
- Don't complain.
- Bring a solution, or at least an open mind, when you express an issue or problem.

Yes, the learning never stops, and **good enough never is**. Feeling a little overwhelmed about the potential for all that learning? Do you need some inspiration? Just watch the children in your class marvel at the raindrops on the window or the stickiness of tape. Don't think of learning and knowing your stuff as chores. Act like the children, without the tantrums. Think of learning as an opportunity, a privilege, and a great joy. So what's next to becoming a pro? Be on the job.

OPTIMIZE YOUR KNOWLEDGE

1 Use your state licensing guidelines to determine the **educational requirements** for early childhood professionals in your state. List the positions, such as teacher, assistant, or director, and the degree or years of education required. Also find out the number of hours of continuing education you must obtain each year in each position.

____

____

____

____

____

2 Make a list of the **classes or workshops** you have completed in the last year. Also note a workshop, seminar, or class you would like to take.

3 Research the **professional early childhood organizations** in your area and call to learn about their meetings, resources, and enrollment information. Create a chart of the information.

Name of organization	Meetings	Resources	Enrollment process and cost

STEP 4

Be on the Job

4

I am prepared for work by being physically present and mentally engaged.

- Always
- Usually
- Sometimes
- Never

What Does It Mean to Be on the Job?

What does being on the job really mean? *Being on the job* means being physically and mentally present, and a bit more than that. *Being on the job* is all about your attitude toward your job, how you connect with people, and how they connect with you. Let's face it: even though being an early childhood professional is a great job, it is still a job. Working with children is the means by which you make money to care for your own family. And with every job comes the good and the bad. It's good because you enjoy children; it's hard because it's work. Every type of work can be demanding, repetitive, and exhausting at times. If work weren't work, we'd called it shopping or sleeping or watching TV. But it's not; it's work.

Given that most of us have to work, the real questions are "Is this the type of work you want to be doing?" "Do you really want to be an early childhood professional?" You could work somewhere else and possibly make more money. My intention is not to steer you to another career but to challenge you to *be on the job*, to have a positive attitude about early childhood education, and to intentionally connect with the people around you. If you are going to work with young children, do it right!

How Do You Do It Right?

A number of things will make you more professional and successful as an early childhood educator. Remember the early childhood education field is unique because your behavior and actions affect the children you care for each day. If you are serious about working with young children, you have no choice but to have a positive outlook and develop constructive relationships. Make sense? If you are a parent, wouldn't you want your children to be surrounded by people who want to work with young children? When you were a child, wouldn't you have wanted that for yourself? Don't you want positive, encouraging adults working with every child? The big questions: Are you a positive adult, or are you just showing up, being *at* the job, but not *on* the job? Do you have a good attitude? You must.

What You Need to Do to Really Be on the Job

To be on the job, you need to be

- Prepared for your job
- Physically and mentally present
- Approachable and likable
- Able to keep your eyes on the children at all times

Prepared for Your Job: Be Ready for the Day

To be on the job, you have to be at the job, and that means being on time. Early childhood education is a profession in which tardiness cannot be tolerated. Period. You will be late occasionally, but being on time, in the classroom, ready to care for children is your primary concern. Each state sets certain teacher-to-child ratios in its licensing and accreditation standards to ensure quality and more important, safety. When you are late and there is no other coverage, children are in danger. It's that simple. Being on time is covered in step 2. Take a look back if you need a review.

Okay, so you know it's important to be on time, but are you running through the parking lot with a wrinkled shirt and wet hair, just sliding into the classroom as your shift begins? I've got news for you: that's not on time or prepared. On time is being prepared to work in the classroom or at your job when you are scheduled. Prepared means that you've gone to the bathroom, taken off your coat, washed your hands, and are ready to start working.

Here's what it takes to be prepared:

Get a good night's sleep. Being on the job starts long before you ever get to your program. Think about the children—when are they the crankiest? Children are short tempered and frustrated when they are tired. It's more difficult for adults to have a positive attitude and relate well to others, too, when we're tired. Take your job and your health seriously, and make getting enough sleep a priority.

Be professional in appearance. You read in step 1 about how your personal appearance affects how others view you as a professional. I include appearance again here because how you look can improve or diminish your approachability. Are you the kind of person others want to come to for encouragement, comfort, or information?

Arrive before you have to be in the classroom or at your position. Being prepared means giving yourself enough time to settle in before you have to start working. This is a tricky point, because the minute people see you, especially children, they tend to engage with you. You can't exactly walk down the hall and ignore the child who says, "Hi." What are you going to do—say, "Save that thought, kid. I'm not on shift yet"? Allow time for short conversations while you move through the parking lot and building. Once you drive into the parking lot or arrive on the campus, you're on!

Deal with personal issues. Being on the job means staying focused on the children. That's a difficult thing to do when you are concerned with personal issues. If there are problems that require your attention, consider taking a personal day. At other times, you have to be professional enough to push aside your concerns about home life in order to care for the children. Their safety depends on it. It is better to speak with your supervisor and take a few more minutes to address your personal concerns than to head to the classroom and not be able to concentrate.

Turn off your cell phone. There is no reason to use your cell phone for personal calls or text messaging at work. Check your phone at the front office if you have a difficult time fighting the urge. You can't watch children and talk on the phone at the same time.

Put away personal belongings like your coat and handbag. Often you can scarcely get your coat off before people start asking you work-related questions. Consider yourself loved and needed, and allow time for it.

Use the restroom. Getting out of the classroom to go shouldn't be such a chore, but ratios and coverage often create a challenge, or at least a situation in which you have to wait. Start your day off right by heading to the bathroom. It's hard to be positive when you're wiggling around.

Finish any food or drink you may have. Each program has different rules about adults consuming food and beverages. Professionals shouldn't eat or drink on the job unless they are having a meal or snack with the children. In many early childhood programs, it's tempting to pick at food and walk around eating. Don't.

Wash your hands. Hand washing is the single greatest way to reduce the spread of germs. Proper hand washing is a must. There is no excuse for not washing your hands and the children's hands. Encourage the children's family members to do so as well. Read the section on hand washing at the end of this step.

Be mentally present. What does that mean, *be mentally present*? Ever drive your car and feel as if you are on automatic pilot? That's what can happen at work as well. You go through the duties of your job, feeding children, doing an activity, but are you really thinking about the children, observing them, asking them questions, listening to their answers, being mentally in the moment? I hope so.

Put on a smile. One of the best ways to prepare for the day is to smile. Seem silly? Just take a look at the children you work with. They smile spontaneously. What happened to us adults? Were smiles socialized out of us? Now, don't throw on a fake beauty pageant smile, but let others know you are happy to be on the job. If you aren't happy to be on the job, well, you know the answer—get another job! So even if it doesn't come naturally or you don't feel like it, smile anyway, and the good feelings will follow.

Bring a good attitude. What constitutes a good attitude? A person with a good attitude is someone who can favorably respond to all types of situations, even the ones they didn't expect. In all my years in early childhood education, I've never experienced two days that were the same. The only thing that you can be sure of in early childhood education is that every day will be full of surprises. I think that our fast-paced, ever-changing, roller-coaster jobs are why some thrive in the field. If you have a good attitude, you're ready for the ride. There's more on this in the next step.

Physically and Mentally Present: Do You Look Like You're on the Job?

Sometimes actions and body language are so overt that others may wonder, "Does she really want to be here?" When working with young children, you never want to convey, even unintentionally, that you would rather be someplace else. That's unprofessional. Here are some behaviors that may give others the impression that you don't want to be *on* the job or even *at* the job. Are you guilty of any of the following don'ts?

Don't sit around. Sitting or lying on the floor or furniture when children are not around is not a good idea. It's okay to stretch out on your stomach and read a story or chat with children.

Don't have your back to others. Having your back to the children is a safety issue, and having your back to adults is just rude. You should always sit so that you can engage with a small group of children and still see the whole room.

Don't do paperwork for an extended period. When children are present, charting what a child ate or taking attendance is fine. Doing your lesson plan around the children is not, unless they are helping you.

Don't attend only to custodial tasks. Your job involves lots of custodial tasks like putting out cots, restocking supplies, and straightening the room. All of these things have to happen, but you can share the work with others, encourage the children to help, and chat with them while you work.

Don't ignore others when they enter the room. Acknowledging and greeting others when they enter your classroom makes them feel welcomed and comfortable. It's good customer service. Get up and say, "Hello" or at least smile. A section about greeting others appears later in this step.

Don't ignore children. It's possible to care for children and never utter a word. Some caregivers develop an assembly line approach to working with children, but that's not what a professional does. Working with children means engaging in conversations. No, you don't need to chat every minute, but you do need to talk with the children when you are feeding them, clothing them, and helping them in any way.

Don't talk about your personal life. Talking to other adults continually about your personal life when you should be working or engaging with the children is unacceptable. Sure, spend a few minutes chatting about what's going on, but keep your focus on the children.

Don't have a sour face. Nothing says, "I'd rather be somewhere else" more clearly than a person with a frown. Turn your frown . . . no, even I won't say that, but you get the idea. You don't have to be constantly smiling, but if you enjoy your job, you should spend the majority of the day smiling, laughing, and having fun.

Don't make sarcastic remarks. For some of us, making sarcastic comments about the program, the children, their families, or the environment has become a bad habit. Break the habit. Remember what your mother told you? "If you don't have something nice to say, don't say anything at all."

Don't be detached. It's possible to perform your duties without connecting to the people around you, but that's not doing your work. That's being *at* the job, not *on* the job. Early childhood professionals know that their primary job is creating relationships with others, especially children.

Don't be a loner. Some people are more social than others and that's okay, but if you like to stick to yourself, early childhood education is probably not the job for you.

Don't be shy. Many people feel more comfortable working with children than with adults. If this is you, recognize this tendency, and understand that to *be on the job*, you have to work equally well with adults. You can make a more positive impact on the life of child if you develop a relationship with the child's family. Work to become more confident in your conversations with adults. You may have to push yourself to connect.

Don't work in cliques. Working in cliques means interacting with only certain adults. Sure, you are naturally drawn to certain people and you may make some lifelong friends on the job, but don't exclude others from your interactions.

Don't be distant. Intentionally or unintentionally distancing your classroom team from other people or teams is unprofessional. It's wonderful that you get along well with the teachers and children in your room, but remember that you have a responsibility to work with everyone in the program. Get to know others beyond your classroom.

Don't do personal things in the classroom. It is never okay to take care of personal things while you are with the children. These might include brushing your hair, reading a book or magazine, or checking your text messages. Wait until your break and head to a staff area in your building if you have one.

Approachable and Likeable: How Do You Acknowledge and Greet People?

How you acknowledge and greet other people clearly defines your professionalism. Picture people arriving at a party. Some people bounce right in, immediately chatting with others, friends and strangers alike. Others arrive a bit more hesitantly, looking for people they know and things with which they are comfortable. And some want to turn around and bolt. Any of those statements describe how you feel? Those statements can also describe how children, their families, your coworkers, and others may feel when they enter your classroom or program.

Just as people can have different responses to entering a situation, people have different approaches or levels of comfort in greeting others. Some may jump up and immediately start a conversation with whomever enters their room, others may dread visitors because they view them as a distraction or feel a bit anxious themselves, while still others are intimidated or afraid of interacting with particular adults, such as demanding parents. Despite how you feel, acknowledging and greeting others remains part of your job, and there's no way around it.

Keep Your Eyes on the Children

Acknowledging others is an important aspect of professionalism. You need to make each child and parent feel special while maintaining the supervision of the other children in the room. Acknowledgment means touching base with a person. It doesn't necessarily mean that you have a conversation right then or that you answer all of his questions. If you are supervising children, it is appropriate and professional to tell parents you will speak with them later. Here are two examples of what you might say:

- "I'd love to chat with you more, but I need to give my full attention to the children. When are you available to talk?"
- "I want to answer your question right now, but I really need to watch the children. May I call you in a little while?"

In this way, you acknowledge the person, keep your focus on the safety of the children, and respond by saying you will be in touch as soon as you're available. Your responsiveness lets the person know

- I see you.
- I hear you.
- I understand you.
- I will schedule an opportunity to speak with you further.

Tips for Greeting Others with Enthusiasm and Professionalism

Here are some tips to help you feel more confident when you are greeting others and a few ideas for even the friendliest among us:

- Make acknowledging others a priority.
- Give your full attention to the child or parent by being prepared. Being prepared means that you have attended to your own needs and organized your classroom so you can focus on others. Being prepared might include washing your hands, stowing away your personal belongings, and putting out activities and toys for the children.
- Give the person your time if you aren't directly supervising children.
- When possible, have enough staff members present so one teacher can greet and the other can supervise the room.
- Look people in the eye. Turn toward arriving adults and greet children on their eye level. You may need to kneel down to greet toddlers or preschoolers.
- Greet people by name and with a smile.
- Introduce yourself and ask others' names if you do not know them. (You should know the names of all the children in your care and their family members.)
- Show your personality.
- Try making physical contact with children and adults who feel comfortable with it. Hug children or gently touch the arm or shoulder of a child or adult.
- Shake hands. With children, say "Hello" in a special way with a high five or a funny handshake. Children like ritual and routine. It gives them something to anticipate and feel special about.
- Start conversations. Tell people you are glad they are here or ask them questions to start conversations.
- Avoid judging families whose children have a hard time separating. Clingy children don't necessarily result from overprotective parents, and being a bit shy is not a fault.

Hand Washing

When children learn and play in your program, they spread laughter, smiles, and, unfortunately, germs. Children like to touch everything, and that includes other people. Even though they're growing up, they tend to put things besides food in their mouths. What's the best way to cut down on germs? Hand washing. Hand washing for the children, their family members, and, of course, you. Hand-washing wipes and disinfectant gel work in a pinch when you are off-site, but running water is a must. When should you wash your hands?

- When you enter a classroom (yours or someone else's)
- Before handling food
- After using the restroom
- After helping a child with toileting
- After coughing or sneezing
- After using disposable gloves
- Anytime you come in contact with blood, urine, or other bodily fluids
- After helping a child wipe his nose

How should you wash your hands? You might be thinking, "I'm an adult. I know how to wash my hands." Believe it or not, many of us don't wash our hands correctly. Here are the ABC's of handwashing:

A. Wet hands with water and then add soap.

B. Use friction to wash your hands for ten to twenty seconds. That's not just a finger dip in the water.

C. Dry with a disposable paper towel and use the towel to turn off the water.

winning ways

So what does being on the job really mean? Here's a quick review. Being on the job means coming to work when you are scheduled and arriving early enough to begin your work on time. Being on the job is also more than that; it's having a good attitude, conveying through words and actions that you enjoy working with young children and their families and that you want to be there. It's no secret to the children, the parents, or others when you lack the enthusiasm and energy to do a good job. Even you know it. Be on the job, or perhaps it's time to get another job.

If you're committed to early childhood education as your career choice, here's the next step to greater professionalism: Save the Comments. Read the next step to find out what Save the Comments is all about.

OPTIMIZE YOUR KNOWLEDGE

1 Interview a teacher or administrator to find out what he or she considers to be the **most important attributes** of an early childhood professional. Also, ask what behaviors he or she considers inappropriate or harmful to the collegiality of the teaching team and the credibility of the program.

2 Describe the way in which early childhood professionals should **greet** children and their families. What behaviors, including body language and gestures, indicate that an early childhood professional is not mentally on the job?

STEP 5

Save the Comments

5

I have a good attitude at work and show it through my actions and conversations.

- Always
- Usually
- Sometimes
- Never

Are You the Real Deal?

Everyone in early childhood education agrees that they love the children, and that may be where complete agreement ends. Until spending time in the classroom, many don't realize that the picture they painted in their heads of working independently with a group of cute, well-behaved kids isn't the real scenario. Yes, the kids are cute! But unlike an elementary school teacher, who usually teaches by herself in a contained classroom, early childhood professionals interact as much with the other adults in the classroom, the program, and the children's family members as they do with the children. So what does all this mean? To be successful in early childhood education, you have to love and work well with children and adults, even though the adults aren't as cute.

Do You Have a Good Attitude at Work?

Do you have a good attitude at work, or do you tend to grumble, complain, and make unfavorable comments? What constitutes a good attitude? A person with a good attitude is someone who can favorably respond to all types of situations. A person with a good attitude

1. Knows and expects that things won't always go as planned
2. Accepts the situation as it is and works to improve it
3. Is generally happy, despite the circumstances
4. Helps without being asked
5. Doesn't look for someone to blame when things go wrong
6. Doesn't always have to be right
7. Works hard and enjoys it

Save the Comments

Look at the preceding statements. Do they describe you, or do you share negative comments about your job and the situations that happen each day? Yes, there are times when you need to professionally articulate your concerns, but people with good attitudes express their emotions without being negative. They express their opinion in order to improve things, not just to point them out. In fact, most people with positive attitudes fix things without drawing attention to the issue or taking credit for the solution. People with good attitudes save the comments. Sure, they feel frustrated, angry, and unappreciated at times, but they move past those feelings and keep the goal of caring for and educating young children in mind. Do you have a good attitude?

What Are the Bad Attitude Don'ts?

I've described the traits of people who have good attitudes; now I'm going to share some of the characteristics of people with bad attitudes. The funny thing, or the not-so-funny thing about people with bad attitudes, is that their behavior can be like a cold: other people can catch it. Hang out with people who have bad attitudes, who always complain, and you'll easily start to pick up some of their traits. The saying, *one bad apple spoils the bunch* makes a lot of sense when you apply it to a team of teachers. Someone with a bad attitude and a big mouth can quickly pull down the whole group. Don't tolerate that negative behavior from others. Don't do it yourself. Don't let yourself be influenced.

The Bad Attitude Checklist

Are you guilty of any of the beliefs or behaviors listed below?

- You want others to hear your opinion about almost everything.
- You don't listen to some people.
- Sometimes you are thinking about what you are going to say next instead of listening to others.
- Sometimes you raise your voice or speak more curtly if others don't hear you or don't agree with you.
- You monopolize the conversations and don't let others talk.
- You need to have the last word.
- You think that no one ever sees your point of view.
- You like it when people tell you that you are right.
- Sometimes you talk to adults as if they are children because you think that will help them understand you.

- You are smarter than everyone else.
- You're never wrong.
- If you were wrong, you would never admit it.
- People say you are hard to get along with, but they are the ones who are hard to get along with.
- You believe that crises are constantly happening at work.
- For as long as you have worked, there have always been problems.
- Sometimes you have to make a scene for others to get your point.
- You take personally things other people say or do.
- No one ever does things the right way, as you would do them.
- You are always the one doing all the work.
- No one ever pays any attention to you.

Do You Give Your Attention to Others?

It's easier to have a good attitude when you direct attention away from yourself and focus on the needs of others. No more complaining or "poor me" attitudes allowed. You took a position in early childhood education to help young children, but contrary to what most people think, it's not the responsibility of your employer or your supervisor or anyone else to make you happy—that's your job. Your employers don't owe you; you owe them. Now, don't misunderstand me, you should never be treated with disrespect or work in an environment that is physically or emotionally unsafe for the children or you. But we tend to focus on our own needs rather than the needs of others. Keep your focus on the kids, and you're likely to have a better attitude.

Take Care of Yourself

In order to focus on the needs of children, you have to take care of yourself. So what's the difference between taking care of yourself and focusing on yourself? A person who is taking care of herself realizes that she has to be physically and emotionally healthy in order to care for others. A person who is focusing on herself thinks primarily about how situations affect her, the same way a toddler sees the world revolving around him. Early childhood education is a demanding profession, and it's easy to become tired and burned out. For tips on how to take care of yourself, check out step 4, Take Care of Yourself, in another book in the *Winning Ways for Early Childhood Professionals* series, *Becoming a Team Player*.

How Can You Be More Positive?

It's easy to complain—everyone does it sometimes. But what if you don't complain, or at least try not to? Being positive does not mean overlooking issues in your program that need addressing. It's important to point out problems in a professional way and solve them as a team. You can say things like, "I don't like the food" or "The paper towels aren't very soft," "The pay is low," and "Some parents don't appreciate us." All of those statements may be true, but do they really matter? If they matter enough, work to change them.

I'm going to take on a sticky subject: salary. You and everyone else know that salaries in early childhood education should be higher in most cases. I have often heard early childhood professionals say, "I don't get paid enough to do all this." Sometimes people are just venting, but at other times, they are using their salary as an excuse for not working as hard as they could or for not doing their job as well as they should.

I'm going to make a tough comment. You knew your salary when you took the job and you agreed to it. Should we work as a field to improve salaries? You bet. Should you slack off or use your wages as an excuse for not getting the job done? Never.

Drop the Negative, Say the Positive

It's very easy for people to be judgmental, to make comments, and to have something to say about almost everything. Here's the challenge to becoming more positive: every time you start to say something negative, switch it around and say something positive. Don't even let the negative come out of your mouth. This is how it goes: "I don't like the food here" becomes "I am so glad we are able to serve meals to the children here." Dropping the negative and saying the positive is going to be a complete change in the way you think. Instead of the first thing that comes out of your mouth being negative, make it positive. If you can't be that positive yet, that's okay—just don't say the negative. Save the comment. Every time you hear yourself start to complain—about a parent, about the equipment, about the pay—stop.

Now, let's take this one more step. Not only are you going to be positive and professional, you are going to help others be positive and professional. When you hear someone say something negative, say something positive. I realize that being overtly positive might not be a part of your natural tendency or personality, and it takes you out of your comfort zone. Push yourself. Make being positive a habit.

Look at the following negative comments, then write a positive one you could say instead.

- **I don't like the slide on the playground.**

  ____

- **We need more colors of construction paper.**

  ____

- **I had to park in the last spot in the lot.**

  ____

- **I won't eat the food from the center.**

  ____

Are Things Really That Bad?

Some programs have a great need for many resources: facility, staff, equipment, and in some places, even food and clothing for the children. Is that the case in your center, or have you lost sight of the abundance of resources that you to use on a daily basis? Do you have a fish tank in your center? Do the children participate in water play? Compared to many parts of the world, your center probably has more water in its fish tanks than most children have to drink on a regular basis. Am I tugging at your heartstrings? I really want to.

Your center, like all early childhood programs, may need some improvements or even a lot of improvements, but let's focus on the positive first. What are the things you enjoy about your program or your job? Write five positive statements about your job.

1 ______________________________

2 ______________________________

3 ______________________________

4 ______________________________

5 ______________________________

How Do You Stay Positive All Week Long?

You can admit that by the time the end of the week rolls around, you're ready for a break. If the quality of your performance has been 100 percent, you're entitled to a "thank goodness." A *thank goodness it's Friday* mentality is understandable, but communicating this to all the families and the children isn't. Imagine that you are being waited on at a restaurant and the server says, "Oh, thank goodness you're my last table." That comment doesn't exactly make you feel as if you can leisurely enjoy your meal, talk with your friends, and have fun. That comment says, "Hurry up and eat. I want to get out of here."

Are you guilty of doing the same thing around families and children? Think of some of these seemingly innocuous statements uttered in front of children or their families.

Thank Goodness It's Friday Comments

- I can't wait until my shift is over.
- Is it time to leave?
- When is this child's mother going to come?
- Your mommy's late again.
- Your dad forgot your gloves.
- That child is here from open to close.
- I'm so tired.
- I need a break.

These comments may not seem so bad, but think about them again. When you make a negative comment about a child's family member in front of the child, how does that make the child feel? Saying, "Your dad forgot your gloves" may make the child feel that you do not like his parent or that you are angry with his parent or even "If my daddy loved me as much as the other daddies love their children, he would have brought my gloves." Children can't control the actions of their family members. When you make negative comments about parents or family members in front of their children, you potentially harm the children, and that's not what you want to do. Best advice: save the comment.

How about a simple statement like "I need a break"? You may very well need and deserve a break, but saying that in front of the children and their family members may make them question your enthusiasm for your job, your attentiveness, or the willingness of the administrators to provide you with a break. Did you mean all that? Most likely not, but negative statements are often misunderstood by others, blown out of proportion, and lead people to question your professionalism. What do you do? You know the answer: save the comments.

Are You Flexible?

Having a good attitude means being flexible. Being flexible means being open to change, and people are creatures of routine and habit. Even good change takes some getting used to for most of us. Think about these questions: Do you like to sit in generally the same seat at the movie theater? Do you like to sit in the back? In the middle? Do you have your sight set on the aisle seat? You sit in the same place in the movie, park in relatively the same area when you go shopping, and sleep on the same side of the bed almost your entire life. Are you flexible? Not really.

I've got a few exercises:

- **If you have on a watch or bracelet, take it off. Now put the watch or bracelet back on, but put it on the other hand. Can you do it?**
- **Write your name in the space.**

  ....

  Now write your name with your other hand on this line.

  ....

  Hard to do?
- **If you have on a jacket or sweater, take it off. Now put the jacket or sweater back on, but put the opposite arm in the sleeve first. How does that feel?**

Each one of these exercises is difficult to do. It's different. It feels uncomfortable, and that's because change is hard. People find lots of comfort in doing the same thing in the same way all the time. We resist things that are uncomfortable and awkward. We don't like changing our ways.

Change and Flexibility

Change and flexibility may cause you to

- Feel uncomfortable and awkward
- Make greater effort
- Learn a new skill
- Fail initially

Why is having a good attitude toward change and flexibility important? As I mentioned before, a day in early childhood education is full of surprises. There's an undeniable feeling in the early childhood environment of fluidity and change. Children are growing and learning, and if you are working well with them, you are responding to their cues and learning quite a bit yourself. You should be figuring out new and better ways to do things. Are you ready to have a good attitude and be flexible? Try sitting in a new section of the movie theater. It's a start.

When to Get a New Job

Contrary to what most people think, being happy is not about your circumstances as much as it is about how you choose to respond to them. In other words, you can choose to be happy even when things aren't perfect. You are going to have days when you feel discouraged or unhappy, but if you are consistently unhappy in your job, perhaps you should think about getting a new job. You can't be the best person you can be if you are not where you are supposed to be. On most days, you should be excited about going to work and being there. The children depend on you, and the choice to be happy is yours.

Are you going to choose to be happy, to make the best of things, to have a good attitude? I think if you really enjoy working with young children, your answer will be *yes.* It's hard to be miserable for long if you like being around children. You can take a lesson on loving life from them. Children are almost always happy.

Okay, if you're ready for a true challenge on saving the comments, let's test your positive attitude with the topic of the next step, Take Care. As an early childhood professional, you are not only responsible for caring for children but also for their families. Dealing with challenging children is tough, dealing with challenging parents and families can be even tougher, and the best way to really care for and educate children is to care for and educate their families. Check out the next step, and for more in depth information on partnering with families, read *Partnering with Families,* another book in the *Winning Ways for Early Childhood Professionals* series.

OPTIMIZE YOUR KNOWLEDGE

1 Describe an early childhood professional who has a **good attitude.**

____

____

____

____

2 Observe in a classroom for fifteen minutes and note the **negative phrases** that teachers use. Rewrite those expressions in a positive way.

3 Review the Bad Attitude Checklist on pages 47–48. Describe a situation in which you had a bad attitude and how you could have responded more **positively and professionally.**

STEP 6

Take Care

6

I realize that my job requires me to care for children and their families.

- Always
- Usually
- Sometimes
- Never

Do You Take Care of Children and Their Families?

Finally, a step on interacting with children. That's the main focus of an early childhood professional and what drew most of us to the field: the children. It's important to keep in mind that your job of caring for and educating children is much more successful when you remember that they come with families. Someone has to drop them off! You may not have signed up to work with adults, but if you want to make a positive, lasting impression on the children, you must do so in partnership with their families. Nothing is more significant than your daily human interactions with the children and their families. It's your responsibility to respond to the needs of the children, helping them develop a sense of trust and security. It's also your responsibility to respond to the needs of each child's family by embracing them with sensitivity and patience. Can you do it? If you really love children, you'll love their families too!

Loving the Children

All right, think of that child in your program who makes you smile, the one you find so easy to love. The people in your own family probably know all about that particular child, too, from all the stories you bring home about your interactions with him, the funny things he does or says. Loving that child is easy. Now think about the child—no names—that you don't gravitate to as easily. Developing a relationship with this child takes more effort. Perhaps she is more demanding, needs lots of encouragement to participate in classroom activities, and maybe she doesn't even smell clean. For whatever reason, it's harder to develop a relationship with this particular child. You know the child. Here's the challenge: as you read about improving your relationships with children, keep the child who's hard to love in mind. Why? The first child that you thought of, the one who makes you smile, probably makes the world smile, too, and will be embraced by many adults. The second child who came to mind, the one who is more difficult to interact with, who isn't so enthusiastic, who maybe doesn't smell clean or look attractive, may make that same impression on other adults. You're in the business of loving children—if you can't love her, who can? There is something amazingly wonderful about every child. You need to find it.

Your responsibility as an early childhood professional is to help every child succeed. The first step in accomplishing this goal is to develop a relationship of mutual love and respect. How do you develop a relationship of love and respect with a child?

> **Invest the time.** Give each child your time and attention. (A primary caregiving system is the best way to ensure each child gets the care he needs. Later in this section, you'll learn more about primary care.)
>
> **Make a genuine effort.** Show the child genuine interest by having conversations with her, asking questions, and playing together. Talk to nonverbal children as well.
>
> **Push through the negative emotions.** Make these efforts of care and concern toward the child even if you don't feel emotionally attached. If you faithfully make efforts to connect with her, the emotional attachment will follow.
>
> **Tell the child you care.** Offer encouragement and praise to the child. Every child has positive attributes.
>
> **Talk the child up.** Help other staff members to connect with this child as well. Every child needs love from a variety of people.
>
> **Make the family feel proud.** Tell the family wonderful things about their child. There may be developmental or behavioral topics you need to discuss with them, but don't forget to focus on the child's successes and positive attributes as well.

Do You Use a Primary Caregiving System?

The daily care and education of young children are not easy tasks. They are physically exhausting and emotionally challenging. You must cope with a wide range of circumstances and, at times, no small amount of stress. To provide good care, you must continually focus on the characteristics and experiences of individual children and their families. In other words, your focus must be on creating individualized or custom-fit care within a group setting, and that's no easy task. No cookie-cutter approaches or one-size-fits-all methods. When it comes to children and their families, they're all so different.

One of the best ways to ensure that children and their families receive individualized care is by having a primary caregiving system. Here's what it looks like. Each teacher is assigned a certain number of children for whom she is responsible. This system does not mean that only the assigned teacher cares for the child but that the assigned teacher makes sure that the child and his family are cared for. The primary caregiver is a communicator, an advocate, someone who is just looking out for that child. In a group setting, it's essential to have a system ensuring that no child falls between the cracks.

The Primary Caregiver's Role

Good care and education happen more easily when each child has a primary caregiver. The primary caregiver should

- Care for each child in a warm and affectionate way that best suits the child's personality and temperament
- Build a relationship with the child's family
- Work with the other staff to make sure the child has a positive experience and that the program meets all of his needs

Because the primary caregiving system is not an exclusive teacher-child relationship, it is also important to develop program goals that support the primary care system. You can't be at the program from open to close, or you shouldn't be, especially if you are working in child care. So how does the primary caregiving system work when you are not around?

winning ways

Consistent Care and Education

Children need predictable, consistent care. Consistent care starts with using a primary care system and is enhanced by making sure that you

- Provide personalized, individualized care for each child
- Develop a care and education plan for each child based on the input of her family
- Have another staff member assigned as the child's primary caregiver when the primary is not present
- Have familiar faces at drop-off times
- Develop staff-to-staff communication strategies
- Help children and their families connect to center staff beyond those in their classroom

Some of the things a primary caregiver should be doing for her primary children are listed below. Read each statement and think about the children in your classroom, then circle your response. If you use a primary care system already, focus on those children. If not, think about the whole class. Make sure that all children and their families are recognized and have an advocate to ensure a positive experience for everyone.

1 I make all the children feel special and help their day go well.

Always Usually Sometimes Never

2 I make families feel special and positive about their children.

Always Usually Sometimes Never

3 I keep other coworkers who are caring for the children up to date on specific information pertinent to the care of the children.

Always Usually Sometimes Never

4 I write Daily Experience Sheets or journal entries, paying particular attention to the information each parent desires. I write comments that convey to parents that their child was engaged, nurtured, and appreciated.

Always Usually Sometimes Never

5 I meet with the lead teacher or director to discuss each child's development and program experience and the family's experience.

Always Usually Sometimes Never

6 I plan appropriate, individual experiences for each child.

Always Usually Sometimes Never

7 I develop a positive relationship and effective communication with families.

Always Usually Sometimes Never

8 I introduce family members to other staff.

Always Usually Sometimes Never

9 I participate in parent conferences.

Always Usually Sometimes Never

10 I am an advocate on behalf of the children and their families.

Always Usually Sometimes Never

How well are you doing? In group care, it's hard to make sure that all children and their families get the care and attention they need. That's what the primary care system is all about. Here are some ideas to help you ensure that all the children and their families receive individualized care.

Individualized Care

How do you individualize care when there are so many little ones to take care of? Here's a partial list of things you need to know about the children in your primary care and in your classrooms. You should commit some of this information to memory; other information can be listed on charts or recorded in other systems to keep you informed. Creating communication and information systems is only the first step to providing individualized care. Keeping the information up-to-date and accurate is an essential second step. What should you know?

About the Child

- Full name
- Age
- Daily schedule
- Developmental skills and abilities
- Special needs
- Individual personality traits
- Interests
- Food preferences
- Food sensitivities and allergies
- Diapering and toileting needs
- Sleeping needs and preferences
- Preferred play and learning experiences
- Effective discipline methods

About the Family Members

- Full name
- Appropriate name for addressing each adult family member

- Contact numbers
- Typical schedule
- Nutritional expectations for child
- Sleep expectations for child
- Diapering and toileting expectations for child
- Academic expectations for child
- Daily information about child provided by parents
- Sensitive issues that may affect the child
- Daily information about the child that parents expect from you

Guiding Children's Behavior

Many new teachers come to the early childhood field expecting children to already know how to socialize and behave, so the teachers can *teach* them. It's often a sobering experience to learn that one of your biggest responsibilities is to teach children how to socialize and behave. It's easy to forget that children are learning all the time. Direct instruction, which most people view as teaching, is only a minor part of working with young children. The first approach to successful discipline is preventing problems before they happen by setting up children to succeed. It's the child's job to push the boundaries and test the limits. It's your job to keep the children safe, help them make the right choices, and gently guide them back within the boundaries when they step over the line.

Helping Children Succeed

Contrary to what many think, discipline is not about punishment but about helping children learn self-control. Children have a better chance of succeeding when you

Establish a program routine. A routine gives children structure, which fosters feelings of security, comfort, trust, and less anticipatory anxiety. When children know what to expect, they feel more in control and can learn and behave more easily.

Have developmentally appropriate expectations. When children aren't behaving, the first thing you should ask yourself is "Can they do what we expect?" Children can't sit or wait for long. Neither can adults. Have you ever run through a yellow light trying to avoid sitting at a thirty second stoplight?

Be consistent. Children understand cause and effect, *first this, then this.* For infants, *first I cry, then someone comes.* For toddlers, *first I hit, then I get the toy.* Children can also learn, *first I ask, then I get the toy.*

Offer children choices when possible. You expect children to make the right choices, but so often you strictly dictate their actions. When you dictate their actions, you're not allowing them to make their own choices, even small ones. "Would you like to sit in a chair or on the floor for group time?"

Convey direction in a positive way. Children need to know *what not to do* as well as *what they should do.* For most early childhood professionals, it's more natural to tell children all of the things they shouldn't do, the "no's," instead of what they should do. Try to direct children using positive words, so they know how to behave correctly. "Please walk instead of running. Please use a quiet inside voice."

Allow for mistakes and forgiveness. Trying to behave is tough work. The children and you will make the wrong choices sometimes. Encourage them to use their words to express how they feel—and you should do the same.

Have consequences for inappropriate behavior. The consequences should be immediate and logical. If children are throwing toys, try to help them use the toys properly or give them an item they can throw safely. If they are still unable to comply, redirect them to another activity.

Love children the most when they misbehave the worst. It's the children who are struggling to gain self-control who need your assistance the most. They can be so disruptive to your classrooms. They zap your time and energy, but they desperately need your love and attention. All children, at all times, including at their most challenging moments, deserve your respect.

16 Don'ts When Disciplining Children

Think about the number of times children like to hear the same book read aloud or push a cart back and forth. Children enjoy repetition. It should come as no surprise that they may need to be guided to make the right choice many times before they do it on their own. You may have to remind them "Please use your walking feet" hundreds of times.

The repetitive behaviors of children can test your patience. Take a break from the classroom if you feel yourself becoming angry or frustrated with the children. In the same way that your encouragement and love can help them succeed, your inappropriate anger and unkind words can hurt them. That is never acceptable. Here is a list of other actions that are unacceptable.

1. Putting a child in the corner of a room
2. Making a child do something to indicate shame, such as wearing a special sign or hat
3. Hurting a child's feelings
4. Being rude to a child
5. Making fun of a child
6. Calling a child names
7. Singling out a child in a negative way
8. Yelling at a child
9. Shaking, shoving, or hitting a child
10. Forcing a child to sit for long periods of time
11. Never giving a child an opportunity to talk
12. Calling a child *bad* and making him feel that he, instead of his behavior, is *bad*
13. Getting personally angry at a child
14. Saying "no" or "stop that" all the time
15. Using food, candy, or fun activities as bribes
16. Withholding food, candy, or fun activities as punishment

How Do You Care for Families?

I stated previously that to give the children the very best care, you have to care for their families too. How does that work? If you're like most early childhood teachers, you didn't take any classes on caring for families. Here's a mini-lesson. Refer to the book *Partnering with Families* in the *Winning Ways for Early Childhood Professionals* series for an in-depth study of working with families.

Don't Judge Families

It's easy to judge the actions and choices of families when they rush in and out every day, but do you really know their intentions and the lives they live beyond your program walls? For example, take this father who appeared to have a hard time balancing work and family. He spent lots of hours on the job and little time at home with his children. Some people thought he didn't care very much. This father grew up poor and was determined to provide his children with a good home and most important, with college educations.

You see, this man was the first person in his family to go to college, and he paid his own way. He wanted his children to go to college as well, but without the financial burden. All three of his children attended college. Today, he sometimes feels guilty about not spending more time with his children when they were little. How do I know? He's my dad. Good parent? The best! Tough choices? You bet.

Drop the "Us" and "Them" Mentality

If you are a parent, you realize that at times there is nothing rational or predictable about being a parent and wanting the best for your child. But even those who are parents quickly forget the parent perspective when they are caring for other people's children. Most parents aren't out to get you or to take advantage of you by running late, forgetting to fill out forms, or showing up with sick children. No, most of those parents are just busy and unorganized like the rest of us. Should we all slow down, spend more time with the family, and get our acts together? Sure, but until the world stops spinning so fast, what can you do as an early childhood professional to help the parents?

- Be patient with the parents.
- Give them the benefit of the doubt.
- Just listen, even when they are angry.
- Help them even when you don't want to.

It's not *you*, the early childhood professionals, against *them*, the parents, or the other way around. When you help the parent, you help the child, and isn't that what everyone wants?

Understanding Parents

- Parents have their children for a lifetime. You have their children only for a few years at most.
- Parents are experts on their children. You might know what to do with the parent's information about the child, but no one knows a child better than his parents.
- Parents love their children more than you do. You may not think so from the choices they make, but they do care more.
- Parents want their children to get an education. You might think that parents are too pushy about academics, but they just want their child to succeed. You can guide parents to the best way to educate children.
- Parents want you to like their children. You can admit that some children are easier to love than others, but you can choose to find the good in every child and communicate that to their parents.
- Parents want you to think that they are good parents. You may not believe that parents care what you think, but they do. Encourage parents in their role. Parenting is hard.
- Parents need your help. You should help them more than you really want to, even when they don't ask.

Ways to Connect with Parents

A true partnership with parents isn't based on telling them what to do and they do it or asking them to raise money for the school. A true partnership is based on sharing information, discussing the best ways to care for the children and run the program, and acting upon their suggestions and input. Many centers do a good job of responding to parents' concerns when there's a problem, and that's good. But let's take it a step further: what if you were to be responsive to family needs before they became problems? What if you were to anticipate the parents' needs and provide for them before the families asked? What if you were to ask parents how you could help them and then you helped? Sound like a lot of work? Excellence is always hard. If you know that caring for families, not just the child, is good for the child, then how can you not do it? Here's how to get started:

1. Know the first and last names of the parents and other adults in the family.
2. Talk to the parents about their children.
3. Introduce yourself to parents and other family members you haven't met.
4. Tell the parents positive things about their children. Think about examples of what the children said, did, or made at school.

Ways to Tell the Parents Good Stuff about Their Children

- Talk to the parent at the beginning or end of the day.
- Leave a voice mail at work or at home.
- Send an e-mail from their child. Include a picture.
- Fax a note to their hotel if they travel.
- Send greeting cards for birthdays, promotions, get well, and just because.
- Put a note in their child's backpack.
- Be available to listen to parents if they want to talk. (If you're not able to do this because you are in the classroom supervising other children, schedule another time that works for you and the parents.)
- Develop a professional relationship with each parent.
- Ask parents what they are thinking. Use a variety of ways to solicit their input.

How to Know What Parents Are Thinking

- **Ask parents.**
- **Call parents at work or home.**
- **Have a parent representative group.**
- **Use a two-minute survey.**
- **Provide an annual parent survey.**
- **Conduct parent/teacher conferences often.**
- **Call parents after they leave the program.**
- **Act upon their suggestions when possible.**
- **Care for the parents and the children.**

Whether you work as a preschool teacher, a child care provider, a family child care provider, a nursery school teacher, or just a plain teacher, you are an early childhood professional, and children and their families deserve your best efforts. As you have just learned, many areas of competency require your professional commitment, from the way you dress to how you act. Your professionalism depends upon how you present yourself to others through your appearance, your communication, your knowledge of the field, the quality of your work, the relationships you develop with others, your work ethic, your determination and dedication, and most important, your attitude. With a good attitude and a willingness to learn, you can easily become a professional, and that helps everyone, especially the children.

OPTIMIZE YOUR KNOWLEDGE

1 Explain the importance of **helping** a child's family in order to better help the child. Without using names, describe a situation in which you can better meet the needs of a particular family. Develop a plan to help them.

2 Describe the **primary caregiving system** and its benefits.

3 Observe a child who is testing limits and record your observations here. Create a **strategy** for helping that child enjoy his experience by being more successful.

Certificate of Achievement

This certificate is presented to

____

for completing the professional development program:

Winning Ways for Early Childhood Professionals: Being a Professional

__________ In-service hours

Redleaf Press®
www.redleafpress.org
800-423-8309

Gigi Schweikert
www.gigischweikert.com

The author and Redleaf Press have not verified the actual completion of the program by this participant.